The Wonder Wedding

Matthew 22: God Chooses

CATHERINE MACKENZIE
Illustrated by Chiara Bertelli

Learn it: God invites you to his kingdom
CF4•K   **Do it: Pay attention to God's Word**
Find it: Who will give you rest? Matthew 11:28

Imagine that you have received an invitation to a feast. It's not just any feast. It's a wedding feast. And it's not just a wedding feast, it's a royal wedding feast. In fact, it's the king's son who is getting married and you've been invited. Would you be excited? Of course, you would!

Jesus told a story about a great wedding feast. A prince was getting married. The king sent out his servants to gather in the guests, but the guests were unwilling to come. How strange! There was going to be delicious food and great fun but they still said, 'No'.

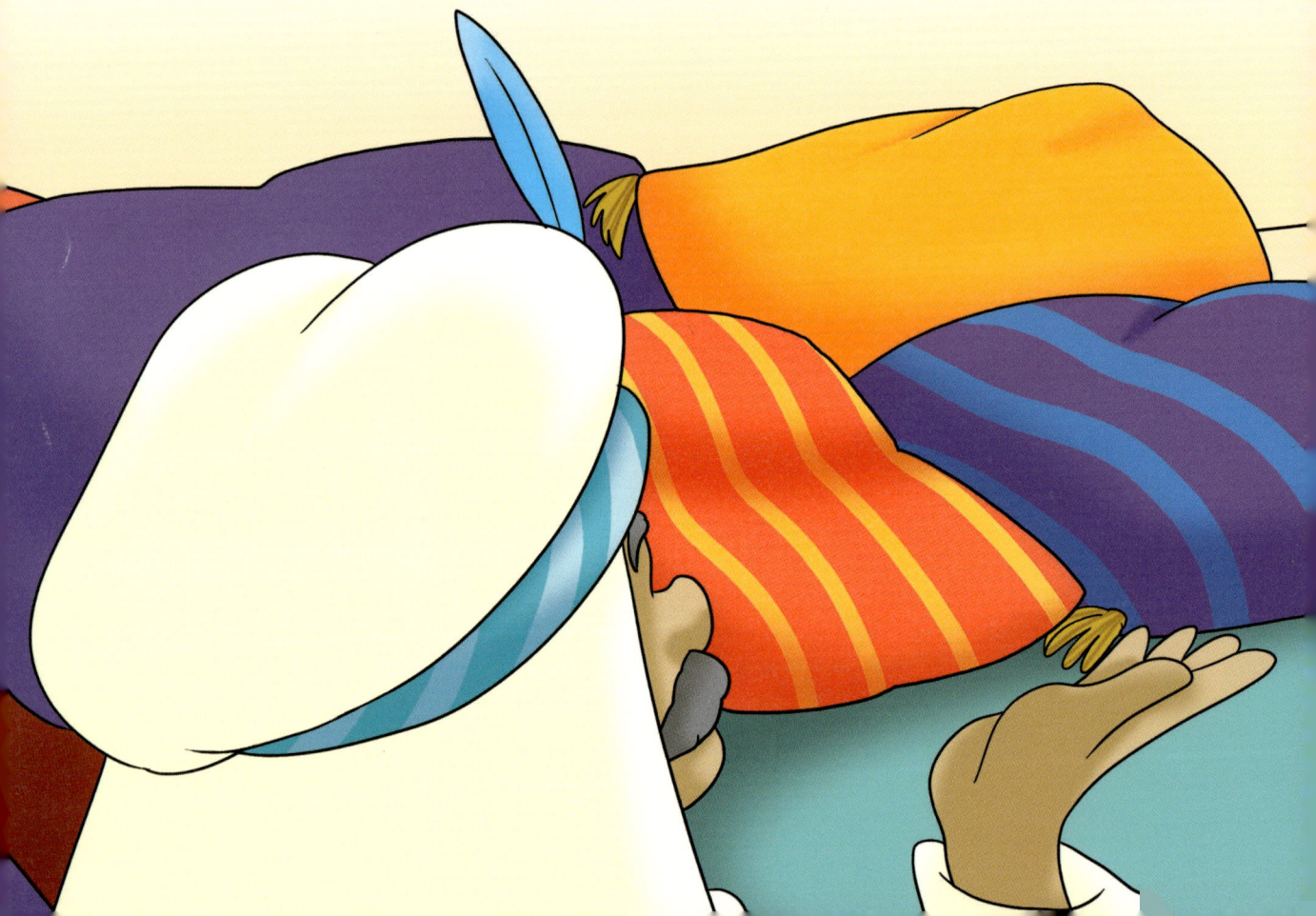

Some ignored the invitation. Others made excuses.

 'I've just bought a field. I can't come.' 'I've just bought some oxen. I can't come.' 'I've just got married. I can't come either.'

The king sent out his servants to invite other people instead and when there were still spaces left he invited even more. Those who said, 'yes' were welcomed with open arms. Soon the feast was filled with people.

The guests were even offered special wedding clothes to wear! What a treat!

However, one man thought his own clothes were absolutely fine. He thought he was good enough! The king asked him, 'Why aren't you dressed properly?' The man made no reply, so he was thrown out of the feast.

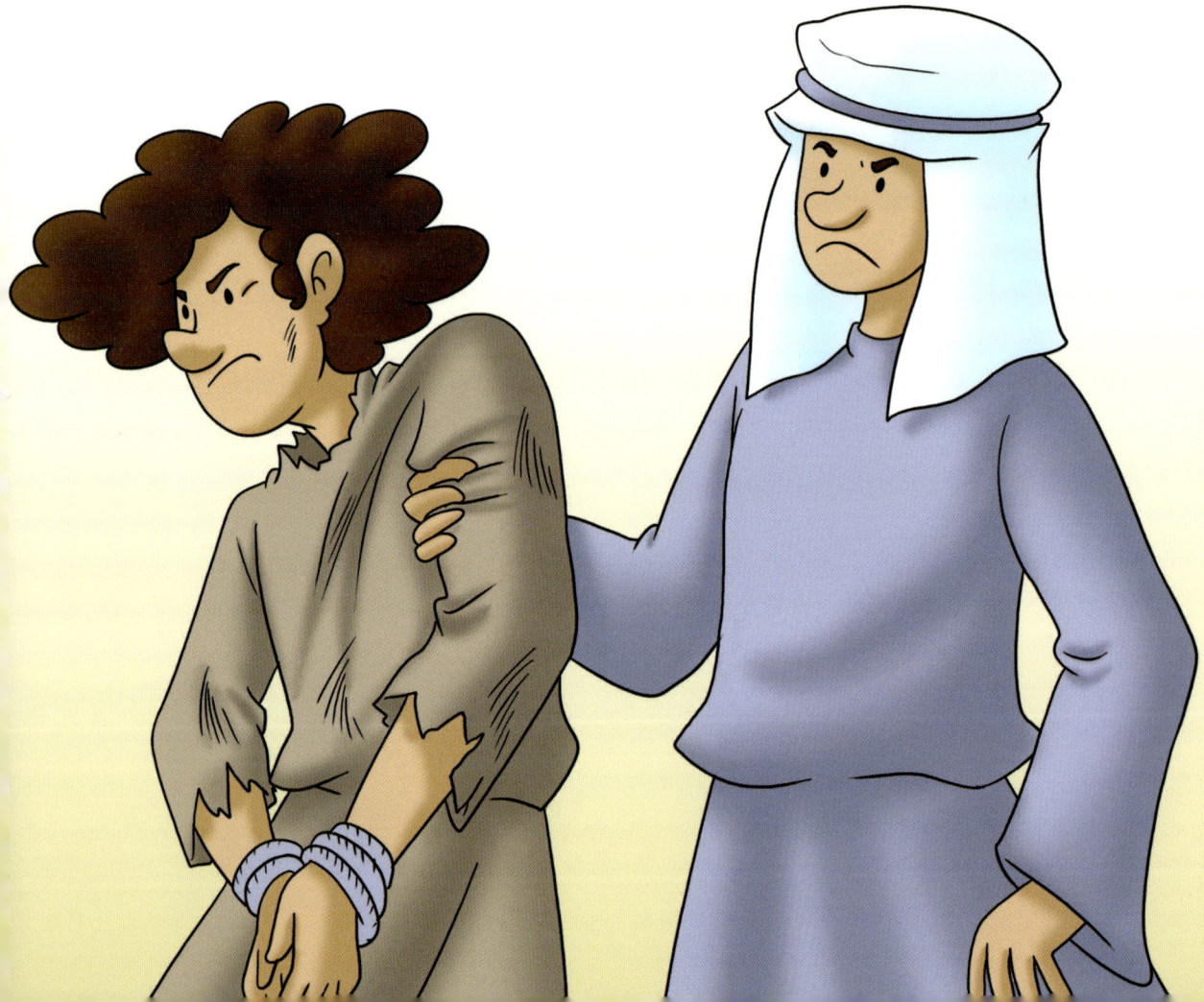

What does Jesus want us to learn from this story? Well, he wants you to know that the Kingdom of God is the best celebration ever. God invites everybody to come, but not everybody will be there.

Some people are like the guests who made excuses. They don't think God is special, so they ignore his invitation. Others are like the man who turned up to the feast in shabby clothes. They don't think God is special either. They want all the good things from heaven, but they don't want to give their life to God.

However, some people say, 'yes' to God. They know he is special. They ask God to forgive them for being disobedient and he does. That's when the celebration starts! The angels in heaven rejoice.

Those who love and trust God want to live lives that please God. They also want others to know how wonderful God is.

One day those who trust God will be with God. One day the celebration will get even better. If you are God's friend, when you die you will go to live with God in heaven. There is no sin in heaven so everything is perfect. It's always joyful, always loving, always peaceful.

WHAT IS SIN? Sin is when you do anything that is disobedient to God. It's when you do, think or say things he says you shouldn't. It's when you don't do, think or say things God says you should.

It's hard to imagine what heaven is like, because heaven is so much better than the happiest, loveliest, most perfect day you've ever had.

If you were asked to a royal wedding would you say, 'No, I'm too busy'? Of course not! You'd do everything to make sure you could go. Would you turn up to the wedding just wearing pyjamas? Of course not! Weddings are special events and everyone tries to look their best. You would want to look your best too.

So remember that God is inviting you to be part of his special celebration. He wants you to be part of his kingdom. Don't ignore his invitation. Say, 'yes'. But when you say, 'yes', you should mean it. Don't just say 'yes' because you want all the good things in heaven. Say 'yes' because God loves you, and you love him and want to please him.

God must be the most important person in your life. It is God who changes people so that they love him and want to obey him. He does this for free. However, just because it costs you nothing to get to heaven, doesn't mean that you do nothing.

You need to be sorry for your sin. You need to trust in Jesus and you need to tell God how wonderful he is. If you don't want to do these things then God hasn't changed you – yet. You haven't really said, 'yes' to God. Ask God to change you now. You've been invited to God's kingdom. Don't ignore your invitation.

Christian Focus Publications

Christian Focus Publications publishes books for adults and children under its four main imprints: Christian Focus, CF4K, Mentor and Christian Heritage. Our books reflect our conviction that God's Word is reliable and Jesus is the way to know him, and live for ever with him. Our children's list includes a Sunday School curriculum that covers pre-school to early teens, and puzzle and activity books. We also publish personal and family devotional titles, biographies and inspirational stories that children will love. If you are looking for quality Bible teaching for children then we have an excellent range of Bible stories and age-specific theological books. From pre-school board books to teenage apologetics, we have it covered!

AUTHOR'S DEDICATON: To my friends and family at Kingsview Christian Centre, A.P.C.

CF4•K
Because you're never
too young to know Jesus

CHRISTIAN FOCUS PUBLICATIONS
Christian Focus · Christian Heritage · CF4K · Mentor

10 9 8 7 6 5 4 3 2 1
Copyright © 2017 Catherine Mackenzie
ISBN: 978-1-5271-0095-4
Published in 2017 by Christian Focus Publications Ltd.
Geanies House, Fearn, Tain, Ross-shire, IV20 1TW, Great Britain
Illustrations by Chiara Bertelli
Cover Design: Sarah Korvemaker
Printed in Malta